MICHIGAN TURTLES AND LIZARDS

A Field Guide and Pocket Reference

James H. Harding

and

J. Alan Holman

Michigan State University Museum

Photography and illustrations by James H. Harding, except where otherwise credited.

FIRST EDITION 1990

INTRODUCTION

There were turtles and lizards before there were dinosaurs, and despite the dinosaurs' demise some 65 million years ago, there are still turtles and lizards today. Though little changed from prehistoric ancestors, these reptiles remain successful animals in the modern world. This book covers the 10 turtle and 2 lizard species that live in Michigan.*

This book is a practical guide for landowners, recreationists, students, educators, wildlife managers, naturalists, and others who would like to identify the turtles or lizards they encounter in Michigan.

To help the reader understand and appreciate these fascinating animals, information on their anatomy, fossil history, habitats, behavior, distribution, captive care, and conservation are also included. On page 11 is a glossary of selected words used in the text or keys. On page 93 is a list of recommended references for more information about reptiles of the Great Lakes area.

---

*The state's 17 species of snakes were covered in the book *Michigan Snakes (Cooperative Extension Service E-2000, 1989)*.

To identify a turtle or lizard, compare it with the photographs in the species accounts. The text description notes the size, shape, and coloration for each species. Another way to identify a specimen is to use the Simplified Keys beginning on page 8 for turtles and page 10 for lizards.

Once you have tentatively identified a specimen, check the range map to see if it is known to occur in the area where you observed or captured it. If it doesn't, you may have misidentified the specimen. Turtles and lizards are sometimes found in areas where they were previously unknown, but animals found out of their known range may have been moved by humans.

If you find a population of a turtle or lizard species that is beyond the range shown in the map, try to take clear photographs of one or more specimens, and note the location as carefully as possible. Report your find to the authors, other herpetologists, or the Michigan Department of Natural Resources. Your observations could be important!

Acknowledgments

The information in this book was obtained from many sources, including the authors' field notes and published data on Michigan and Great Lakes turtles and lizards. The regional publications by Ruthven et al. (1928), Minton (1972), and Vogt (1981) were particularly helpful, as was the general reference edited by Halliday and Adler (1986).

The range maps are based on those in Conant (1975) but have been updated and modified on the basis of specimens in the collections of the Museum of Zoology, University of Michigan, and the MSU Museum, Michigan State University, as well as the authors' field notes. However, these maps are not intended for establishing precise species distributions or range extensions. Where the reports are questionable, the areas are shaded in light color. Photographs not otherwise credited were taken by James H. Harding.

Dr. James Gillingham, of Central Michigan University, generously provided data on the newly discovered Tuscola County population of six-lined racerunners. Mr. Peter Wilson, of Eaton Rapids, shared unpublished reproductive data on several Michigan turtle species. Dr. Ned Fogle, of the Fisheries Division, Michigan Department of Natural Resources, provided information on the laws and regulations relating to reptiles. Many other herpetologists offered information and encouragement.

We are grateful to members of the Department of Outreach Communications at Michigan State Universisty, who helped publish this guide. Comments and criticisms are welcome.

CHECKLIST OF MICHIGAN TURTLES AND LIZARDS

CLASS *Reptilia* (Reptiles)

ORDER *Testudines* (Turtles and Tortoises)

SUBORDER *Cryptodira* (Straight-Necked Turtles)

FAMILY *Chelydridae* (Snapping Turtles)

☐ Snapping Turtle *(Chelydra serpentina)* **Page 12**

FAMILY *Kinosternidae* (Musk and Mud Turtles)

☐ Common Musk Turtle *(Sternotherus odoratus)* **Page 16**

FAMILY *Emydidae* (Pond and Box Turtles)

☐ Spotted Turtle *(Clemmys guttata)* **Page 20**

☐ Wood Turtle *(Clemmys insculpta)* **Page 24**

☐ Eastern Box Turtle *(Terrapene carolina carolina)* **Page 28**

☐ Blanding's Turtle *(Emydoidea blandingii)* **Page 32**

☐ Common Map Turtle *(Graptemys geographica)*
Page 36

☐ Painted Turtle *(Chrysemys picta)* **Page 40**

☐ Red-Eared Slider
(Trachemys scripta elegans) **Page 44**

FAMILY *Trionychidae* **(Softshell Turtles)**

☐ Spiny Softshell *(Apalone [= Trionyx] spinifera)*
Page 48

Lizards

ORDER *Squamata* **(Lizards and Snakes)**

SUBORDER *Sauria* **(Lizards)**

FAMILY *Scincidae* **(Skinks)**

☐ Five-Lined Skink *(Eumeces fasciatus)* **Page 52**

FAMILY *Teiidae* **(Whiptails and Racerunners)**

☐ Six-Lined Racerunner *(Cnemidophorus sexlineatus)* **Page 56**

Characteristics of Michigan Turtles

These silhouettes represent adult female specimens of the ten species of Michigan turtles drawn to scale to show comparative sizes. Adult male map and spiny softshell turtles are also included, as there is a great size difference between the sexes in these species. Just under 10% of natural size.

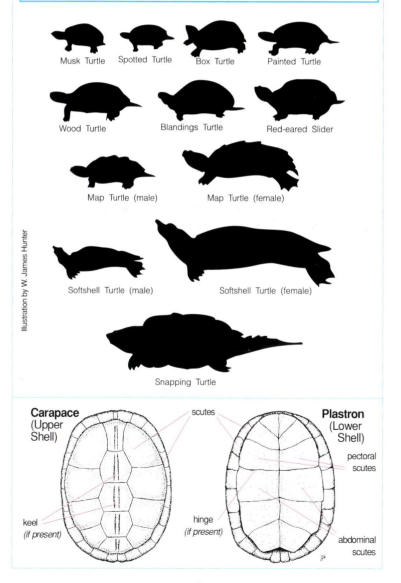

Illustration by W. James Hunter

Musk Turtle · Spotted Turtle · Box Turtle · Painted Turtle
Wood Turtle · Blandings Turtle · Red-eared Slider
Map Turtle (male) · Map Turtle (female)
Softshell Turtle (male) · Softshell Turtle (female)
Snapping Turtle

Carapace (Upper Shell) — scutes, keel (if present)

Plastron (Lower Shell) — pectoral scutes, hinge (if present), abdominal scutes

Simplified Key to the Turtles of Michigan

To use this key, start at the first set of paired descriptions and compare the two sets of characteristics given. Choose the one (a or b) that better fits the turtle and proceed to the next number indicated and compare those two. By this process of elimination, you will eventually arrive at the name of the animal and where to find the species account. *The illustrations on page 7 and the definitions on page 11 will help you use this key.*

1. a. Shell rigid and covered by scutes **GO TO 2.**

   b. Shell flexible at edges and covered by leathery skin

   Spiny Softshell *(Apalone spinifera).* **See page 48.**

2. a. Less than 12 scutes on the plastron **GO TO 3.**

   b. 12 scutes on the plastron **GO TO 4.**

3. a. Tail very long, with large triangular scales along the top; plastron small and cross-shaped

   Snapping Turtle *(Chelydra serpentina).* **See page 12.**

   b. Tail short, without large triangular scales on top; plastron small, with skin between some scutes; usually two yellow stripes on side of head

   Common Musk Turtle *(Sternotherus odoratus).* **See page 16.**

4. a. Plastron with a hinge between the pectoral and abdominal scutes **GO TO 5.**

   b. Plastron without a hinge **GO TO 6.**

5. a. Upper jaw terminally hooked; carapace domed, with a central keel

   Eastern Box Turtle *(Terrapene c. carolina).* **See page 28.**

b. Upper jaw terminally notched; carapace usually smooth and unkeeled; chin and throat yellow in color

Blanding's Turtle *(Emydoidea blandingii)*. **See page 32.**

6. a. Head and neck with narrow stripes **GO TO 7.**

b. Head and neck without narrow stripes **GO TO 9.**

7. a. Edges of carapace usually marked with red; carapace smooth and unkeeled; rear edge of carapace not strongly serrated

Painted Turtle *(Chrysemys picta)*. **See page 40.**

b. No red markings on edges of carapace; rear edge of carapace usually serrated **GO TO 8.**

8. a. Yellow spot behind eye; plastron unmarked or with dark lines along the scute edges; carapace often with fine light markings

Common Map Turtle *(Graptemys geographica)*. **See page 36.**

b. Red or orange stripe behind each eye; plastron with a rounded dark blotch in most or all scutes, or (old males) infused with dark coloration

Red-Eared Slider *(Trachemys scripta elegans)*. **See page 44.**

9. a. Head black above with rounded yellow or orange spots; carapace smooth and dark (usually black) with variable number of rounded yellow spots

Spotted Turtle *(Clemmys guttata)*. **See page 20.**

b. Head black, usually without yellow spots; rough brownish carapace with distinct growth rings

Wood Turtle *(Clemmys insculpta)*. **See page 24.**

KEY TO MICHIGAN LIZARDS

To use this key, start at the first set of paired descriptions and compare the two sets of characteristics given. Choose the one (a or b) that better fits the specimen and proceed to the next number indicated and compare those two. By this process of elimination, you will arrive at the name of the animal and the page number of its species account.

1. a. Skin smooth, without scales; no claws on toes

   This is not a lizard! (It is a salamander, which is an amphibian and not covered in this book.)

   b. Skin covered with small scales; sharp claws on toes **GO TO 2.**

2. a. Smooth scales on body and tail; belly scales about the same size as back scales; five stripes on back (if stripes are present)

   Five-Lined Skink *(Eumeces fasciatus)*. **See page 52.**

   b. Dull scales on body, rough scales on tail; belly scales rectangular and wide and larger than back scales; six stripes on back

   Six-lined Racerunner *(Cnemidophorus sexlineatus)*. **See page 56.**

Like most salamanders, this eastern tiger salamander has smooth skin and no claws.

This six-lined racerunner, like nearly all lizards, has a dry scaly skin and sharp claws

Selected Terms Used in Key and Text:

aquatic—living in water.

barbel—a fleshy, often pointed projection of skin on the chin or throat of some turtles.

blotch—an irregular spot or patch of color.

carnivore—an animal that feeds on other animals.

carapace—the top part of a turtle's shell.

cloaca—a chamber just before the anal opening.

elliptical—oval in shape.

herbivore—animal that feeds mostly on plants or plant products.

hinge—a flexible division between two parts of the bottom shell (plastron) of certain turtle species that allows one or both parts of the shell to move up and down.

keel— a raised ridge (or ridges) running lengthwise down the carapace of some turtles.

omnivore—an animal that feeds on both plants and animals.

plastron—the bottom part of a turtle's shell.

population—the members of a species (a recognized group of plants or animals) living in a specific geographical area.

predator—an animal that kills and eats other animals.

scute—one of the large scales on a turtle's shell.

serrated—having pointed projections along the edge.

spherical—rounded in shape, like a ball or globe.

vertebrate—animals with backbones and (usually) a bony skeleton.

Snapping Turtle
(Chelydra serpentina)

DESCRIPTION:

This large aquatic turtle has a big head with a pointed nose and hooked upper jaw, and a long, thick tail with a row of large, triangular scales along the top. The carapace is black, brown, gray, or olive, with pointed marginal scutes along the rear edge. (The shell is often covered with algae or mud.)

Young snappers have three lengthwise keels on the carapace, but large adults may have shells that are nearly smooth. The yellowish plastron is small and cross-shaped and leaves much of the turtle's underside uncovered. This lack of protection may partly explain the snapping turtle's well-known biting defense.

This is Michigan's largest turtle, often reaching 10 to 35 pounds (4.5 to 16 kg); the record weight was 86 pounds (39 kg) for a captive specimen. Adult carapace length: 8 to 18.5 inches (20 to 47 cm).

DISTRIBUTION AND STATUS:

■ Found throughout Michigan, except Isle Royale, this species is generally common, but many local populations have been reduced by exploitation. The Michigan Department of Natural Resources (DNR) regulates the taking of snapping turtles with closed seasons, size limits, daily and possession limits, and licensing and trapping regulations. Always check with the DNR for current rules before trapping or capturing turtles.

SNAPPING TURTLE

The small plastron (left) of the snapping turtle may explain its biting defense.

Adult snapping turtle.

HABITAT AND HABITS:

■ Snapping turtles occur in a variety of aquatic habitats but are most common in slow-moving rivers, marshes, and muddy-bottomed lakes with dense plant growth. They seem quite tolerant of organic pollution. Snappers rarely bask but frequently travel overland when seeking better habitat or nesting sites, and many are killed while crossing roads.

These turtles are particularly aggressive when out of water, not hesitating to strike out at humans or any other potential enemy. The snapper's long, powerful neck and sharp jaws can deliver a damaging bite. When under water, snapping turtles rarely bite unless restrained, preferring instead to hide in the mud or swim away.

The only safe way to carry a large snapper is to grab the base of the tail, making sure the head is pointed away from your body and other people. This method can injure the turtle's tail vertebrae, however, and a miscalculation could result in injury to the handler as well. *It is best to leave these animals alone whenever possible.*

■ Snapping turtles eat a variety of foods, including insects, worms, leeches, crayfish, snails, tadpoles, frogs, fish, birds, small mammals, carrion, and a variety of aquatic plants. All food is eaten underwater. Contrary to popular belief, these turtles do not harm game fish populations under natural conditions. Large snappers sometimes take young ducks and geese, but the effect of such predation on overall waterfowl numbers is minimal. (Predators such as raccoons, foxes, skunks, and certain large fish may have a greater impact on waterfowl reproduction.)

Only in small, intensively managed fish or waterfowl breeding areas would control of snapping turtle numbers be beneficial. They are important members of the wetland ecosystem, and routine persecution is unjustified. This is the turtle species most in demand for meat and for making turtle soup.

■ Most breeding activity occurs in the spring and early summer; female snappers may remain fertile for several years after mating. Nesting takes place from late May into July (mostly in June.) The female seeks a sunny site with moist sand or soil, sometimes traveling a considerable distance from the water. In marshes they will often nest in muskrat houses or on dikes or road edges. From 10 to 96 spherical eggs, looking something like Ping-Pong balls, are buried in the nest. Larger females lay more and larger eggs.

Predators destroy many nests. Those eggs that survive hatch in 55 to 125 days. Hatchlings are black, 1 to 1.5 inches (2.5 to 3.8 cm) in carapace length, with very long tails. Despite their instincts to hide and to give off a musky odor and "play dead" when touched, few hatchlings survive to adulthood.

Hatchling (right) and-one-year old (left) snapping turtles.

Common Musk Turtle
(Sternotherus odoratus)

DESCRIPTION:

This is a very small turtle with a narrow, high-arched brown or black carapace and a pointed, protruding snout. They usually have two yellowish stripes on each side of the head. (In older specimens these stripes may fade.) Two or more soft, pointed barbels are usually visible on the chin or throat. The yellow or brownish plastron is very small, with many of the scutes separated by skin. The male musk turtle differs from the female in having broader areas of skin between the plastral scutes and a longer, thicker tail tipped with a stiff spine. Adult carapace length: 3.25 to 5.37 inches (8.3 to 13.6 cm).

DISTRIBUTION AND STATUS:

■ Musk turtles are locally common in the southern half of the Lower Peninsula; records exist for the northern half, but are not confirmed. This species is distributed rather unevenly through its Michigan range.

HABITAT AND HABITS:

■ These turtles inhabit shallow, slow-moving or quiet waters with some aquatic vegetation. In Michigan they prefer the shallows of lakes with marl, sand, or gravel bottoms. Poor swimmers, they usually crawl along the bottom, nosing under or around objects for food. Musk turtles rarely bask out of water but may occasionally climb out onto rocks or emergent branches to sun themselves. During the warmer

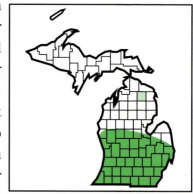

COMMON MUSK TURTLE

Note the algae growth on the carapace of this adult musk turtle (above).

When disturbed, musk turtles give off an unpleasant odor, earning them the nickname "stinkpot".

The very small plastron has skin between some of the scutes.

months they are most active in the early morning and in the evening, and some populations are quite nocturnal. When disturbed, musk turtles give off an unpleasant musky odor from glands under the edge of their shells. This has led to the common name "stinkpot". They will also threaten with open jaws and bite if handled.

Musk turtles eat a wide assortment of foods, always underwater. Included in their diet are insects, snails, crayfish, worms, tadpoles, and aquatic plants.

■ Female musk turtles nest from May to August. Some dig a normal nest cavity, but others simply deposit their eggs under shoreline debris or fallen logs, or in the sides of muskrat houses. Each female lays from 2 to 9 elliptical, brittle, hard-shelled eggs. These hatch in 60 to 80 days into tiny black hatchlings less than an inch long. Those lucky enough to reach adulthood may live for many decades. The record for a captive was over 54 years.

The eggs of the common musk turtle are brittle like birds' eggs.

The stripes on this musk turtle's head may fade with age. Note the barbel visible under its chin.

Spotted Turtle
(Clemmys guttata)

DESCRIPTION:

The little spotted turtle has a smooth, black carapace with a variable number of rounded yellow spots. The plastron is yellow or orange with a black blotch in each scute. The blotches may cover most of the plastron in some specimens. The head, neck, and legs are black above, usually with a few scattered yellow spots, and there are usually one or more irregular orange or yellow bands on the side of the head. The skin under the legs and neck is orange or pinkish. Occasional specimens have no spots on the carapace; others may have only one spot per scute. Males usually have brown eyes and brown or black lower jaws, while most females have orange eyes and yellow or orange lower jaws. Adult carapace length: 3.5 to 5 inches (9 to 12.7 cm).

DISTRIBUTION AND STATUS:

■ Spotted turtles have been recorded from most of the Lower Peninsula, except for the northeastern counties and the northern tip of the Thumb, but are most common in the southwestern corner of the Lower Peninsula. Destruction of their specialized wetland habitat and exploitation by pet collectors have led to a serious decline in their numbers over much of the state, and the species is generally rare and confined to localized colonies.

■ ***The spotted turtle is listed as a species of special concern by the Michigan Depart-***

SPOTTED TURTLE

The spotted turtle's spots help it blend in with its habitat. (See the cover of this book.) Note that the number of spots can vary from turtle to turtle.

The plastron is yellow or orange with a black blotch in each scute, but the black may cover most of the plastron.

Photo by P. Wilson

ment of Natural Resources. *This turtle is protected by state regulations and may not be taken from the wild or possessed without a scientific collector's permit issued by the DNR.*

HABITAT AND HABITS:

■ This species inhabits small ponds, bogs, sphagnum seepages, and grassy marshes. The primary requirements are clean, shallow water with a mud bottom and ample aquatic and emergent vegetation.

Spotted turtles become active quite early in spring and often bask on logs or grass clumps. If disturbed, they dive into the water and hide in mud or aquatic vegetation. Overland movement is common. These turtles are not often seen in summer. They are less active in hot weather, and the growth of surrounding vegetation helps to conceal them. Shy and retiring, spotted turtles rarely bite in self-defense.

■ Spotted turtles eat a variety of small animals and plants, including insects, snails, worms, slugs, crayfish, tadpoles, duckweed, algae, and fruit. Most food is taken and eaten underwater.

■ Mating usually occurs in April and May in shallow water. Males pursue the females, nipping at their legs and shell margins; they may also fight with other males courting the same female.

In June, females move to elevated, open places to nest. From 2 to 7 elliptical, soft-shelled eggs are buried in the nest cavity. Incubation can take from 45 to 83 days, depending on nest temperature and humidity. Hatchlings usually have black carapaces with one yellow spot per scute. An occasional hatchling will have a brownish carapace without spots, but nearly all have some spots on the head.

Photo by R. D. Bartlett

Spotted turtles prefer small ponds, bogs and sphagnum seepages as habitat.

Athough most hatchlings are born with spots, some are spotless (lower left).

This little spotted turtle is about a year old (lower right).

Wood Turtle
(Clemmys insculpta)

DESCRIPTION:

The scientific name of this species means sculptured turtle, and its rough, brownish carapace does look as if it was carved from wood. Each scute has deep, circular growth rings crossed by ray-like ridges. The plastron is yellow with a black blotch at the outer edge of each scute and has a V-shaped notch at the base of the tail. The head and upper legs are mostly black or dark brown (rarely speckled with yellow or white), while the neck, lower legs, and other soft parts are yellow or orange. Mature males have higher shells and longer, thicker tails than females. Adult carapace length: 6.3 to 9.4 inches (16 to 24 cm).

DISTRIBUTION AND STATUS:

■ Wood turtles occur in the northern Lower Peninsula and the Upper Peninsula. Scattered records from the southern LP may represent released specimens. These turtles can be locally common in suitable habitat with minimal human disturbance, but many populations have declined significantly over the past two or three decades. Collecting wood turtles for pets has significantly reduced some populations. Many wood turtles are killed on roads built near northern rivers. This species may be more threatened by being directly exploited and accidentally destroyed by humans than from loss of habitat.

■ The Wood Turtle is listed as a species of special concern by the Michigan Depart-

WOOD TURTLE

Plastron of a wood turtle (above).

The head of the female wood turtle (top) is narrower than that of the male (middle right).

The annuli (growth rings) can be used to estimate the age of a wood turtle until it is about 15-20 years old.

ment of Natural Resources. **They are protected by state wildlife regulations and may not be taken from the wild or possessed without a scientific collector's permit issued by the DNR.**

HABITAT AND HABITS:

■ Wood turtles occur in and near rivers and streams of the north woods. They prefer streams with sandy bottoms and avoid rocky sections with fast current. These turtles often bask on logs or grassy banks. They may wander through adjacent swamps, woods, and meadows, especially in summer, but are never far from moving water. Most wood turtles inhabit a rather small home range, living much of their lives (perhaps 40 years or more) within a few acres.

Wood turtles depend largely on concealment for protection and rarely bite. When leaving the water, they often throw sand or dirt over their shells with quick backward strokes of the front feet, helping them to blend with their surroundings. Lacking the protective plastral hinge of the box turtle, wood turtles are quite vulnerable when on land, and specimens are often found with one or more limbs missing due to attacks by predators. The ability of some turtles to survive such crippling injuries is noteworthy.

■ Wood turtles feed (both in and out of water) on insects, worms, slugs, snails, carrion, algae, berries, willow leaves, and numerous other items. Some specimens have been observed capturing worms by thumping the ground with the forefeet or plastron; the vibration apparently disturbs the worms and brings them to the surface.

■ Courtship and mating can occur from spring through fall. Courting behavior may include a "dance" in which the male and female face each other and swing their heads from

Turtles construct their nests with their rear legs and never see their own eggs (top). Wood turtle eggs hatch in 45-80 days. Note the caruncle (egg tooth) on the hatchling that is used to slice open the egg (below right).

side to side. Later the male may climb onto the female's shell, gripping the edges with his claws, and repeatedly strike her carapace with his plastron. Mating usually takes place in water on a sloping stream bank.

Most females nest in June, burying from 4 to 18 elliptical eggs in an open, sunny location. Incubation can take from 45 to 80 days, depending on nest temperatures and humidity. Many nests are lost to predators, particularly raccoons. The brown or gray hatchlings have long thin tails and lack the yellow or orange skin color of the adults and older juveniles. They may grow from a hatching carapace length of about 1.25 inches (3.2 cm) to an adult size of about 6.3 inches (16 cm) in 12 to 15 years in a favorable environment, but few hatchlings survive to adulthood.

■ In wood turtles the number of growth rings (annuli) in each scute can be used to determine an approximate age for juvenile and young adult specimens, but this method becomes much less reliable for turtles over 20 years old.

Eastern Box Turtle
(Terrapene carolina carolina)

DESCRIPTION:

This is a small land turtle with a domed carapace and a hinged plastron. Coloration of the shell and skin is extremely variable. The carapace is usually brown with a radiating pattern of yellow or orange markings in each scute. The plastron can be yellowish, tan, brown, or black, and either plain or marked with lines or blotches. Skin of the head and legs is usually brown or black with streaks and spots of yellow, but some (especially males) may have the yellow or orange color covering most of the head and forelimbs. The plastral hinge allows the box turtle to close the shell tightly, completely hiding the head, legs, and tail. Most male box turtles have red eyes, while most females have brown eyes. Adult carapace length: 4.5 to 7.8 inches (11.4 to 19.8 cm).

DISTRIBUTION AND STATUS:

■ Eastern box turtles have been found in the southern and western Lower Peninsula. They are locally common in the southwestern counties but have practically disappeared from much of their former Michigan range. Loss of wooded habitat to various human uses is the most serious threat to the species, but many box turtles are killed on roads or collected as pets each year.

■ *Eastern box turtles are listed as a species of special concern by the Michigan Department of Natural Resources.*

EASTERN BOX TURTLE

The gentle eastern box turtle is Michigan's least aquatic turtle, preferring to live in open woodlands.

Plastron (above) showing hinge.
Most male eastern box turtles have red eyes (left).

They are protected by DNR regulations and may not be killed or removed from the wild.

HABITAT AND HABITS:

■ This is Michigan's only truly terrestrial turtle. They typically inhabit open woodlands, often near water, but may wander into thickets, meadows, grassy dunes, and gardens. They will soak at the edges of ponds or streams in hot weather but avoid deep water and swim poorly. Most box turtles remain in a rather small home range (often less than 5 acres) for most of their lives, and they may live a long time — some have reportedly passed the century mark. Well protected by their shells, box turtles rarely bite to defend themselves.

■ Eastern box turtles eat a great variety of plants and small animals, including insects, worms, slugs, snails, carrion, mushrooms, berries, and fruit. The young are largely carnivorous but take more plant foods as they grow. A liking for tomatoes, strawberries, and melons may occasionally attract these gentle creatures to gardens, but they are easily fenced out or transported away from the problem area.

■ Courtship and mating is most frequent in spring but may occur in summer and fall. Courtship behavior involves much nipping and nudging of the female's shell by the male.

Females can lay fertile eggs for up to four years after one mating. Most nesting takes place in June, with 3 to 8 eggs being buried in an open, often elevated location. Incubation requires from 75 to 90 days. Hatchlings are gray or brown with a single yellow spot in each carapace scute. They spend most of their time hiding under leaves and other forest debris and are rarely seen. The plastral hinge does not work in very young box turtles, but they can give off a strong odor that may deter predators.

Mating pair (above).

The eggs of the box turtle have thin, flexible shells.

Hatchlings are gray or brown with one yellow spot in each carapace scute. They are well camouflaged for hiding in the debris of the forest floor.

Blanding's Turtle
(Emydoidea blandingii)

IDENTIFICATION:

Blanding's turtle is a medium-sized turtle with an elongated, dome-like carapace and a long neck. The smooth carapace is usually black with a variable number of yellowish spots and streaks. The head is also dark, with brown or yellow spots, but the chin and the underside of the neck are bright yellow. The yellowish plastron has a dark blotch at the outer edge of each scute, and there is usually a flexible hinge between the pectoral and abdominal scutes. A frightened turtle may use this hinge to lift the front and back of the plastron and close up its shell. Hinge flexibility varies greatly between individuals, and some specimens have little or no shell closing ability. Adult carapace length: 6 to 10.5 inches (15.2 to 26.7 cm).

DISTRIBUTION AND STATUS:

■ This turtle is fairly common in parts of the Lower Peninsula but is rare and local in the Upper Peninsula. Primary threats to the species include loss or altering of wetland habitats and destruction on roads.

HABITAT AND HABITS:

■ Blanding's turtles inhabit shallow bodies of water with some aquatic plant growth and a muddy bottom, such as marshes, ponds, and river backwaters. They are most often seen wandering overland in spring and fall.

BLANDING'S TURTLE

Note the long neck and bright yellow chin that distinguish Blanding's turtle.

The hinge on the plastron allows some Michigan specimens to close up their shells.

Females seeking nest sites may travel considerable distances. Unfortunately, these turtles are frequent road victims.

Blanding's turtles are timid creatures that rarely bite defensively, relying instead on their shells for protection. They are potentially long-lived animals, often living 50 years or more. Most feeding occurs underwater, where prey is captured by a quick thrust of the long neck. Favorite foods include crayfish, insects, tadpoles, frogs, and carrion.

■ Mating occurs in water in the spring. The yellow neck coloration probably assists in species recognition. Most females nest in June, burying from 3 to 21 elliptical, soft-shelled eggs in a sunny location. The hatchlings emerge in late August or September. They have dark gray or brown carapaces averaging about 1.25 inches (3.2 cm) long, and long thin tails.

This Blanding's turtle is less than a year old.

Common Map Turtle
(Graptemys geographica)

IDENTIFICATION:

The map turtle has a greenish, olive, or brown carapace with a low keel and an irregular pattern of yellowish lines that suggest roadways on a map. This pattern may be obscured in older specimens. The skin on the head, neck, and legs is olive or brown with thin yellow stripes, and there is usually a small yellow spot behind each eye. The plastron is light yellow, though young specimens often have dark lines running along the scute edges. Females are larger and have much wider heads than males. Adult female carapace length: 6.7 to 10.7 inches (17 to 27.2 cm). Adult male carapace length: (4 to 6.3 inches (10 to 16 cm).

DISTRIBUTION AND STATUS:

■ Map turtles are found in the southern and western counties of the Lower Peninsula. They are common in many rivers and lakes, but some populations have been reduced or eliminated by pollution or by unthinking persons who use basking turtles as living targets for firearms. (Shooting reptiles is illegal in Michigan.)

HABITAT AND HABITS:

■ Map turtles live in the larger lakes, rivers, and oxbow sloughs, where they are often seen basking on emergent logs and rocks. When disturbed, these shy animals dive into the water and hide under log jams or submerged

COMMON MAP TURTLE

The map turtle has markings resembling a topographical map on its back (top). The plastron is mostly yellow (above).

This map turtle hatchling will head for the water immediately upon emerging from the nest.

brush. Map turtles are powerful swimmers and, unlike most turtle species, will inhabit waters with fairly strong currents.

■ The wide jaws of adult females are well adapted for crushing the shells of snails, other mollusks, and crayfish. The males feed on aquatic insects and smaller mollusks. Feeding takes place underwater.

■ Female map turtles dig their nest holes in sunny spots near the water, often on warm, rainy evenings, from late May to early July. One or two clutches containing from 6 to 20 elliptical eggs are produced each year. The eggs hatch after an incubation period of 65 to 80 days. The hatchlings, about 1.25 inches (3.2 cm) long, head directly for water upon emerging from the ground and can swim and dive well almost immediately. Some hatchlings may overwinter in the nest and emerge in spring.

Painted Turtle
(Chrysemys picta)

DESCRIPTION:

This is a common, small, dark-shelled turtle with a yellow-striped head and red and yellow stripes on the neck, legs, and tail. The smooth black or olive carapace has red markings along the edge, especially underneath the marginal scutes. The plastron is usually yellow, sometimes tinged with red, with a long, dark central blotch. In some specimens this blotch is nearly absent, while in the western subspecies (see Distribution and Status) the blotch is wider and more complicated and extends along the seams between the scutes. (See page 42.) Males are smaller and have longer front claws than females. Adult carapace length: 4 to 7 inches (10 to 18 cm). Record length (western subspecies): 9.8 inches (25 cm).

DISTRIBUTION AND STATUS:

■ Painted turtles are the most common Michigan turtles. Two subspecies occur in the state. The midland painted turtle (*Chrysemys picta marginata*) is found throughout the Lower Peninsula and the eastern and central Upper Peninsula. The western painted turtle (*Chrysemys picta belli*) enters Michigan in the western Upper Peninsula. Many painted turtles in the Upper Peninsula are intermediate between the midland and western forms (determined by the extent of the dark pattern on the plastron; see the illustration on page 42).

PAINTED TURTLE

Basking painted turtle (top).

The long front claws of the male painted turtle are used during courtship (above).

Adult painted turtle, showing head and shell markings (right and above right).

41

HABITAT AND HABITS:

■ Ponds, lakes, marshes, and slow-moving streams and rivers are all homes to painted turtles. They prefer shallow water with a muddy bottom and ample aquatic vegetation and often move overland to find suitable habitat. Many are killed while attempting to cross roads. Painted turtles tolerate organic pollution and survive even in urban areas. Painted turtles feed in water on a variety of foods, including aquatic plants, insects, snails, crayfish, tadpoles, small fish, and carrion.

■ During courtship, a male painted turtle will swim backward in front of his intended mate, tickling her head and neck with his long front claws. Most mating occurs in the spring. Females nest from late May into July, seeking sunny sites with slightly moist sand or soil near the water. The female lays from 4 to 20 (usually 7 or 8) elliptical, soft-shelled eggs in the nest cavity and carefully covers them. The eggs hatch in about 70 to 80 days, but hatchlings from late nests often remain in the ground over the winter and emerge in spring. The inch-long (2.54 cm) hatchlings survive the sub-freezing nest temperatures by producing a type of natural antifreeze in their bodies.

The markings on the plastron of the turtle above identify it as a midland painted turtle. The western subspecies is found in the western Upper Peninsula. Intermediate specimens in the UP show varying degrees of dark coloration on the plastron.

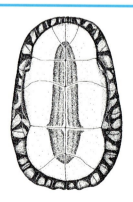

Midland Painted Turtle
(Chrysemys picta marginata)

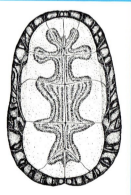

Western Painted Turtle
(Chrysemys picta belli)

Photo of emerging hatchling by W. Leonard

Nesting female painted turtle (nest has been exposed by the photographer).

Hatching occurs in 70 to 80 days (top inset), but the hatchlings may not leave the nest until spring. The plastron pattern often varies in painted turtle hatchlings (bottom inset) where the western and midland subspecies merge in the Upper Peninsula.

Red-Eared Slider
(Trachemys scripta elegans)

DESCRIPTION:

The red-eared slider is named for the broad red or orange stripe behind the eye, which may extend onto the neck. Otherwise, the head, neck, and legs are greenish with yellow stripes. The olive or brown carapace usually has yellow and black longitudinal bands and stripes. The plastron is yellow with a dark, rounded blotch in each scute. Males are slightly smaller than females and have longer claws on the forefeet. Old specimens, especially males, may become very dark, with black coloration obscuring the striped pattern on the skin and shell. Adult carapace length: 5 to 11 inches (12.5 to 27.9 cm).

DISTRIBUTION AND STATUS:

■ This is a common turtle from northwestern Indiana south to Georgia and west to Texas and Oklahoma. Red-eared sliders are probably not native to Michigan, but breeding populations exist locally in the western and southern Lower Peninsula. Many thousands of baby sliders were once imported into this state for the pet trade, so it is likely that released or escaped specimens are responsible for the established colonies. Isolated specimens may turn up almost anywhere in Michigan.

HABITS AND HABITAT:

■ Red-eared sliders prefer to live in still-water habitats (lakes, ponds, sloughs) with abundant aquatic plant growth and nu-

RED-EARED SLIDER

Adult female red-eared slider.

The plastron of older males may be darker than the markings on this turtle.

The red or orange stripe behind the eye gives the red-eared slider its name.

merous basking sites on logs or other emergent objects. These turtles are called sliders because they quickly slide from their basking spots into the water when disturbed.

■ Red-eared sliders feed on aquatic plants and animals such as crayfish, snails, insects and tadpoles, and carrion. The young turtles are mostly carnivorous but eat increasing amounts of vegetation as they get older.

■ Courtship and mating in red-eared sliders take place in water. As in painted turtles, male sliders use their very long front claws to tickle the head and neck of the females during courtship. The females usually nest in June, burying from 4 to 25 elliptical eggs in a sunny location. Incubation takes about 65 to 80 days. The hatchlings are about 1.25 inches (3.2 cm) long and have bright green carapaces with yellow markings. Growth can be rapid, and under ideal conditions sliders may reach breeding size in two to four years.

Spiny Softshell
(Apalone spinifera)

DESCRIPTION:

This medium to large turtle is unmistakable, with its flat, smooth shell and long, pig-like nose. The rounded tan, brown, or olive carapace is marked with black dots or circles in juveniles and males, and dark blotches in adult females. The plastron is white, with gray patches over the plastral bones. Both carapace and plastron lack scutes and are quite soft and flexible. The name "spiny" comes from the small spines at the front of the carapace. The neck is very long, and a yellowish, black-bordered stripe is usually visible on the sides of the head. Females are larger and darker and have shorter tails than males. Adult female carapace length: 7 to 19 inches (18 to 48 cm). Adult male carapace length: 5 to 9 inches (12.7 to 23 cm).

DISTRIBUTION AND STATUS:

■ Softshells are locally common in the southern three-quarters of the Lower Peninsula. Populations in some areas have been reduced or eliminated by water pollution and exploitation by humans. The Department of Natural Resources regulates the taking of spiny softshells with closed seasons, minimum size and possession limits, and special licensing and trapping regulations. Check with the DNR for current rules before capturing these turtles.

HABITAT AND HABITS:

■ These turtles occur in rivers, large lakes, and impoundments; sandy or muddy bottoms

SPINY SOFTSHELL

Adult male spiny softshells (top) retain the juvenile pattern of spots on the carapace. Hatchling spiny softshell (above right). Plastron of adult spiny softshell (above).

Female softshells are much larger than males and darker in color (right).

are favored. They will bask on logs or sloping banks but spend much time buried in sand or mud in shallow water where they can use their snorkel-like noses and long necks to get air. Softshells can breathe underwater by absorbing their oxygen through throat and cloacal linings. This may explain their sensitivity to pollutants that also kill fish.

■ Spiny softshells are sometimes called "leatherbacks" or "pancake" turtles. They are very fast swimmers and are surprisingly agile on land, though they rarely venture from the water except for nesting. Their main defenses are concealment and fast escape. When handled they can deliver a painful bite with their sharp jaws.

■ Crayfish are reported to be the favorite food of this species, though they will also eat aquatic insects, snails, tadpoles, and fish.

■ Most nesting occurs in June, with females seeking open, sunny sites near the water and depositing from 4 to 38 spherical, brittle-shelled eggs in each nest. Most hatchlings emerge in August or September, though some overwinter in the nest and emerge in spring.

When underwater, the spiny softshell's long nose is used like a snorkel, allowing the turtle to get air while submerged.

Five-Lined Skink
(Eumeces fasciatus)

DESCRIPTION:

The skink is a small lizard with smooth, shiny scales. Females and young have 5 yellowish, white, or tan stripes on their backs, and blue tails. The background color is black in young specimens and brownish in adults. In males the stripes fade and may disappear completely, and the tail becomes gray. During the spring breeding season much of the male's head becomes reddish orange, and this color may be retained on the lips and chin throughout the year. Adult length: 5 to 8 inches (12.7 to 20.3 cm).

DISTRIBUTION AND STATUS:

■ Five-lined skinks have been found in most of the Lower Peninsula and the central part of the Upper Peninsula. They are locally common in some areas but rare or non-existent in many other parts of the state with similar habitats. Field surveys are needed to define the present range and status of this lizard in Michigan.

HABITAT AND HABITS:

■ Five-lined skinks are woodland animals, preferring edges and openings where there are stumps, logs, or other objects for cover or basking sites. They may be found in wet or dry habitats. Five-lined skinks are active from late April through early October.

FIVE-LINED SKINK

Photos by W. Leonard

The bluish tail of the juvenile five-lined skink is retained by the adult female (top), but the adult male usually loses the stripes and develops a reddish head (inset).

Basking is used to raise their body temperatures to suitable levels for activity, about 65° to 93° F (18° to 34° C). When temperatures are too cool or hot, skinks remain hidden. Five-lined skinks are fast runners and can move rapidly to cover when threatened.

Photo by W. Leonard

The tail of a skink is easily disjointed, and if a predator grabs it, the tail can be left behind still wiggling to distract the attacker while the lizard escapes. Later a new tail regrows, though it is grayish and shorter than the original.

■ These lizards feed mostly on insects and spiders, though some Michigan skinks have been observed eating berries.

■ The males defend territories by chasing other males; they do not chase the females or young, which may be recognized by their blue tails. Courtship and mating occur in spring. Females lay from 5 to 15 eggs, usually under a log, loose bark, or rotten wood. They curl around their eggs and brood them until they hatch, turning and cleaning them, fending off small predators, and removing rotten eggs. The eggs hatch in one to two months, and the mother may protect the newly hatched skinks until they disperse from the nest.

This juvenile skink is basking to raise its body temperature to a level suitable for activity. It will quickly move to cover if threatened.

Photo by W. Leonard

Six-Lined Racerunner
(Cnemidophorus sexlineatus)

DESCRIPTION:

Six-lined racerunners are slender, long-tailed, brownish lizards with six yellow stripes down the back. The young have light blue tails and brighter coloration than the adults. Racerunners have dull scales, with rings of rough scales around the tail. (The only other Michigan lizard, the five-lined skink, has smooth, shiny scales.) Males may have bluish bellies. Adult length: 6 to 9.5 inches (15.2 to 24.1 cm). Two-thirds of the length is tail.

DISTRIBUTION AND STATUS:

■ The six-lined racerunner is known in Michigan from only one population in Tuscola County. This lizard is widespread in the southeastern and central United States, and it ranges north into Wisconsin and northwestern Indiana. At this time it is unknown whether the Michigan racerunners have been introduced by humans or represent a natural population. Several thousand years ago the climate was warmer and drier than it is today, which could have allowed these lizards to spread into Michigan from Indiana.

Any sighting of six-lined racerunners in the state should be reported to the DNR Wildlife Division and to the Biology Department at Central Michigan University in Mount Pleasant.

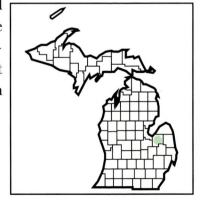

SIX-LINED RACERUNNER

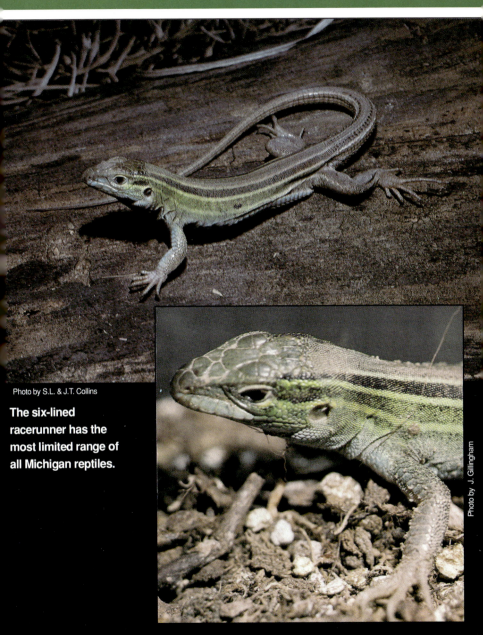

Photo by S.L. & J.T. Collins

The six-lined racerunner has the most limited range of all Michigan reptiles.

Note the ear opening behind and below the eye, a characteristic of most lizards.

HABITAT AND HABITS:

■ These lizards inhabit grasslands, shrubby places, or rocky hillsides with loose, sandy soils. They prefer drier, more open habitats than the five-lined skink. Racerunners take refuge in burrows from excessive heat or cold. They may dig their own or use burrows dug by other animals.

As the name implies, these lizards are very fast runners, escaping predators with a fast dash into a burrow or other shelter.

■ Six-lined racerunners feed on insects, spiders, and other small invertebrates. Like snakes, they frequently stick out their tongues while foraging, probably picking up odor particles that may lead them to food.

■ Females lay from 2 to 8 elliptical eggs in an underground burrow in June; they may lay a second set of eggs later in summer. Unlike skinks, racerunners do not brood their eggs, which hatch in about two months. The young grow quickly and can breed in their first year.

TURTLES, LIZARDS and PEOPLE

*T*urtles and lizards probably have a better public image than their fellow reptiles, the snakes. Few people fear turtles, and many human cultures have looked upon the turtle as a symbol of patience, peace, and long life. The fable of the tortoise and the hare is an example of how turtles are celebrated for their slow and steady nature. Turtles have figured in the folklore and mythology of human cultures over much of the world, particularly in Asia, China, and the Americas. Many creation myths place turtles in prominent roles. Hindu and Chinese traditions describe the Earth as resting on the back of a great turtle, and a number of Native American legends also feature turtles supporting the primordial world. Lizards are perhaps less important in cultural lore, unless we count the dragon as an exaggerated version of these mostly small and inconspicuous reptiles.

■ There are no venomous turtles and few species offer any threat to people. The only venomous lizards are two species from the arid southwestern United States and Mexico. In some parts of the United States, the five-lined skink was thought to be dangerous (and given the dubious local name "scorpion"), perhaps because of the reddish head of the male. Most animals, from chipmunks to chickadees, will bite if handled, and the majority of turtles and lizards are no exception. (On the other hand, some species — like the Blanding's turtle — seem unwilling to bite under any circumstances.)

This Blanding's turtle, rescued from the road and returned to its habitat, depends on its shell for protection. This species rarely, if ever, bites as a defense.

Turtles are ecologically important members of Michigan's fauna and play a particularly prominent role in wetland habitats. Many species are predators on insects and other small animals, and some are scavengers that help recycle dead organisms. Box turtles help disperse seeds of berry-producing plants. Turtles also have an aesthetic value, and many people enjoy seeing them. For instance, a view of turtles peacefully basking on logs adds greatly to the enjoyment of a fishing or canoe trip.

The snapping turtle is undoubtedly Michigan's most economically important species, as it is widely trapped for meat and soup. Spiny softshells are also taken for this purpose, but they are much less common and have a more limited Michigan range.

In some tropical and subtropical areas, lizards are among the most numerous and significant vertebrates. Here in Michigan our two species may have less of an ecological impact, but they are interesting animals that do play a role in nature as consumers of insects and other invertebrates.

Conservation

■ Turtles and lizards have been greatly affected by the changes that humans bring to the natural world. Most turtles depend on water and wetlands, and the loss or degradation of these habitats is particularly significant. It is estimated that nearly 75 percent of the original wetlands in Michigan have been drained, filled, or otherwise destroyed. Rivers, streams, and lakes have been polluted and are often fringed by residential developments. Agricultural expansion, logging, and urban growth have greatly reduced wetland and upland habitats, and in some areas the irresponsible use of off-road vehicles has degraded what remains. The widespread use of chemical pesticides is undoubtedly detrimental to insect-eating species such as the five-lined skink and spotted turtle. It is inevitable that the numbers of turtles and lizards are considerably diminished from what they were only a few decades ago.

■ The direct destruction and exploitation of turtles by people is a serious problem. Hundreds of mature turtles are killed on roads each year, and certain species have been heavily collected as pets (e.g., box, wood, and spotted turtles) or for food (snapping turtles and softshells). This lost adult breeding stock may not be replaced in a population already under stress from habitat reduction or increases in egg predation. (The raccoon, a major predator on turtle eggs and juvenile turtles, has greatly increased its range and numbers in Michigan over the past few decades.) The numbers of these turtles can decline to the point where recovery is difficult or impossible. When coupled with intense exploitation by humans, this decline can be quite rapid. Commercial pet collectors have eliminated targeted turtle species in some places.

Snapping turtle populations may tolerate a limited harvest by individuals taking them for personal use, but their numbers can be rapidly depleted when they are subjected to intensive commercial harvest. Market trapping, unregulated before 1989, has seriously affected snappers in parts of Michigan.

Michigan regulates the taking of native reptiles and amphibians in two ways. Species listed as endangered or threatened under the Endangered Species Act are fully protected. In addition, reptiles can be protected or regulated under the fish and wildlife statutes. For example, wood turtles, spotted turtles, and box turtles are fully protected and cannot be taken from the wild at any time, except with a scientific collector's permit. For all other species, there are limits on the numbers that may be taken or possessed. Both snapping turtles and softshells are protected during closed seasons, and at other times these species are regulated by size limits and trapping restrictions.

The taking of reptiles or amphibians for sale or commercial use requires a separate license, and different limits may apply on certain species. Persons needing to take turtles or lizards for scientific research must apply for a scientific collector's permit. Periodically, new species may be added to the endangered or threatened species list. **Be sure to check with the Department of Natural Resources Fisheries Division for current rules before taking or disturbing any native reptiles or amphibians.**

Notes on Turtle Biology

    Turtles are reptiles, a class of animals that includes lizards, snakes, and crocodilians, as well as extinct fossil groups such as the dinosaurs, the flying pterosaurs, the porpoise-like ichthyosaurs, and many others. Living reptiles are lung-breathing, back-boned animals with dry, horny scales on their skin and claws on their feet (if they have feet!). Most lay shelled eggs on land, though some snakes and lizards give birth to live young. Turtles are by far the most primitive living reptiles and, except for their shells, resemble some of the earliest reptiles known.

A Long History

■ Turtles have been called living fossils, for they were undoubtedly present before the first dinosaurs appeared. The most ancient turtle fossil known lived some 200 million years ago and was much like later turtles except for some extra bones in the shell, a more primitive skull, and teeth in the roof of its mouth (all later turtles were toothless.)

    During the Mesozoic era, the great Age of Dinosaurs, turtles developed into the basic forms that we see today. Softshell turtles, much like those in southern Michigan rivers, lived alongside huge, long-necked dinosaurs like *Diplodocus* and *Apatosaurus*. Ancestors of the familiar hard-shelled pond turtles evolved during the Cretaceous period as the dinosaurs peaked and then dwindled to extinction at the end of the Mesozoic, some

65 million years ago. By the Miocene epoch, about 15 million years ago, painted turtles, sliders, musk turtles, and snapping turtles had appeared.

Turtles (about 250 species) are found on all of the continents except Antarctica and occur in all of the world's oceans. Michigan has nine native turtle species (and one introduced species), which is quite a few for a temperate region. Britain has no turtles, and the whole continent of Europe has only five non-marine species. This situation reflects the fact that glacial ice covered much of the northern United States, Britain, and Europe from time to time over the last million years, until about 14,000 years ago. A vast southern refuge for turtles existed in North America, but the locations of oceans and mountain ranges meant that no such refuge was available in most of Europe. We know that by 6,000 years ago at least five of our native turtles had reinvaded Michigan's Lower Peninsula from the south.

Turtle Architecture

■ Although the word "turtle" can be properly used for all living shelled reptiles, the strictly land-living species are often called tortoises. None of these live in Michigan. (In Britain, the word "tortoise" is used to include freshwater turtles, and "turtle" is used only for ocean species.) All living turtles are classified into two groups: the cryptodires (hidden-neck turtles), which pull their

The Australian snakeneck turtle bends its head sideways to pull it into the shell, as opposed to the hidden-neck turtles (including all Michigan species), which pull their head straight into the shell with a vertical bend in the neck.

heads straight into their shells with a vertical bend in the neck, and the pleurodires (side-neck turtles), which swing their heads under their shells with a sideways bend of the neck. All of Michigan's turtles are cryptodires.

The fossil record shows that several types of reptiles had evolved shells of one kind or another, but turtles were the most successful. All others died out millions of years ago.

The turtle shell is composed of flat plates of bone that are overlain by thin, horny scales called scutes. It includes portions of the backbones, ribs, shoulder skeleton, and bony skin plates. The scutes overlap the seams between the individual bones, giving the shell added strength. The upper shell, called the carapace, is attached to the lower shell, or plastron, by a bony bridge.

Details of shell structure vary considerably between species. The fast-swimming softshell turtles have an incomplete bony shell, covered by leathery skin. Snapping turtles have very small lower shells, allowing greater mobility as they walk along pond and lake bottoms. Not surprisingly, turtles with reduced armor tend to bite readily when confronted by possible predators. On the other hand, the well-protected box turtles rarely bite, since they can completely close their shells using a hinge on the plastron. In the South, cooter turtles have very thick, high-domed shells for protection against the crushing jaws of alligators.

In some turtle species, growth rings (annuli) are visible as a series of circular ridges on the shell scutes. A ring forms each time the turtle stops growing, which in northern species is usually during the winter dormant period. By counting the rings in one scute, it is sometimes possible to estimate the turtle's age. This method is less reliable for older specimens. A turtle's growth slows as it ages and rings formed later in life are small and hard to count. Also, in older turtles the scutes may become worn, obscuring the annuli.

■ Compared with other vertebrates, turtles live long lives. One land tortoise lived in captivity for 152 years and was thought to have been about 200 years old when it died. Eastern box turtles probably hold the age record among Michigan species. They are known to reach 100 years or more. Blanding's and wood turtles can surpass the half-century mark, and even the little painted turtle can live over 20 years. Conversely, a large, algae-covered snapping turtle that looks like an aged centenarian may be less than 30 years old!

The turtle skull is very primitive, being completely roofed over with bone as in the earliest land vertebrates. Muscles that move the jaws are inside the bony roof, leaving little room for the brain, which is quite small. Turtles are toothless, but the jaws are covered by a horny beak that is efficient for grabbing and slicing food. Some turtles that specialize in eating snails and other mollusks have broadened jaw surfaces, which help crush the shells of their prey. Female map turtles, with their greatly widened heads, are noteworthy for this adaptation.

Turtles have a great many adaptations for survival in varying habitats. The structure of their feet, for example, tells us much about their habitats and lifestyles. Land-living tortoises usually have solid, elephant-like feet.

Gopher tortoises of the southeastern United States have flattened shovel-like front feet for digging their long burrows. Our terrestrial box turtle has moderate sized, unwebbed feet that show a close relationship with more aquatic species. Most aquatic species, such as sliders, painted, and map turtles, have webbed hind feet and at least partially webbed front feet to assist in swimming. The softshell turtles have fully webbed feet (and flat, streamlined shells) for efficient movement in water and can swim faster than many freshwater fish.

Other Adaptations

■ As in all reptiles, turtles breathe with lungs, but many aquatic species can also absorb oxygen through their skin, throat linings, and little thin-walled sacs in the cloaca (anal area). Spiny softshells can get much of their oxygen using these alternate breathing methods. (Due in part to their dependence on underwater breathing, softshells are often the only turtles stunned or killed by rotenone, a poisonous chemical used by wildlife managers to kill fish.) Oxygen uptake through throat, skin, or cloaca may also be used by turtles that hibernate underwater during the colder months, when low temperatures greatly decrease oxygen needs. Some turtles are able to survive for long periods under low-oxygen conditions.

■ Turtles are ectothermic (cold-blooded) animals that require outside sources of heat to live and function properly. Active Michigan turtles seem to prefer a body temperature between 72° and 86° F (22° to 30°C), although they can tolerate much lower temperatures and are occasionally seen swimming under ice. Turtles cannot tolerate excessive heat, and most will die if exposed to temperatures over 104° F (40°C).

In winter, aquatic turtles usually burrow into the bottom mud of lakes or rivers, or take refuge in muskrat burrows or other shelter. Land-living turtles dig into leaf litter or other forest debris. They pass the cold months in a dormant (sleep-like) state, with life processes slowed down to minimize energy needs.

At other times of the year, most turtles bask in the sun for varying periods each day to maintain preferred body temperatures. Basking also helps eliminate skin parasites, and sunlight contributes to vitamin D synthesis in the skin of turtles as it does in other animals, including humans. People who see turtles sunning on logs along the edges of rivers and lakes may think that these animals are rather lazy, but basking is an essential behavior for a turtle's well-being.

Food and Feeding

■ Most Michigan turtles are omnivorous, eating both plants and smaller animals. In many species, such as box, wood, painted, and slider turtles, the young are quite carnivorous (meat-eating) but take more vegetable matter as they get older. Other species are largely carnivores throughout their lives. Snapping turtles feed on nearly any small creature that they can capture and also eat carrion (food items already dead.) Blanding's and softshell turtles take a variety of small animals but seem to prefer crustaceans, while map turtles specialize in eating snails. Preferred foods are noted in the account for each species.

Feeding methods vary considerably between species. Most turtles feed in water. Both snapping turtles and softshells may either conceal themselves and lie in ambush for unsuspecting victims or actively stalk their prey. A Blanding's turtle captures small aquatic animals with a quick dart of its long neck. Painted turtles often probe mats of water plants to stir up small prey. They also take in tiny plants and animals by opening their mouths and expanding their throats at the water's surface, allowing the water (and food) to flow in. Many aquatic turtles use a type of gape and suck feeding when lunging at prey. Some turtles are unable to swallow food unless their heads are submerged, including painted, slider, map, softshell, and snapping turtles. Eastern box turtles and wood turtles are the only Michigan species that regularly feed on land, where they look for plants, berries, insects, worms, and other small animals.

Reproduction

■ Telling a male from a female turtle is sometimes difficult, but there are usually visible hints to a turtle's sex, as long as it is a mature specimen that can be closely examined. It helps to have two turtles of opposite sex to compare! The best clue is in the structure of the tail. Male turtles often have somewhat longer, thicker tails than females, with anal openings at or beyond the edge of the carapace when the tail is fully extended. Females generally have smaller tails, with anal openings underneath the edge of the carapace. There are additional clues that work for certain species. In sliders and painted turtles, males have claws on the front feet that are twice as long as the female's. In spotted, wood, box, and Blanding's turtles, most males have a concave plastron (the middle of the plastron looks pushed in.) This depression fits the curvature of the female's carapace during mating. There are sometimes other sex differences, such as size and coloration, and these are noted under the individual species descriptions.

■ Mating behavior can include complicated courtship rituals. A male painted turtle will swim backward in front of its intended mate and vibrate its long foreclaws on the female's face and chin. Red-eared sliders also employ this tickling routine. Wood turtle pairs sometimes do a head-swaying "dance" while facing each other, and other species also use variations on head swaying or bobbing. Male box turtles may bite at the female's legs, head, and shell margins during courtship.

As in all reptiles, fertilization is internal, requiring the male turtle to bring his tail in contact with the female's to allow insertion of the penis. This may require considerable effort by the male. In high-shelled species like the box turtle, the male must cling in a vertical or

Almost all turtle species use similar techniques to build nests. The female turtle digs the nest cavity with her hind legs, lays her eggs and refills the hole. These snapping turtle eggs, uncovered by the photographer, were carefully reburied after the photograph was taken.

backward-tilted position during mating, which presents a special hazard. After mating, a male box turtle can fall backward, and if it should fall on soft soil and be unable to turn back over, it may die. Perhaps it is fortunate that female box turtles, and some other species as well, can lay fertile eggs for three or four years after a mating.

■ All turtles lay eggs, which can be either spherical (rounded) or elongated and oval. In Michigan, only snapping turtles and softshells lay spherical eggs. Turtle eggs may have hard, brittle shells or thin, flexible shells that are easily dented. Most Michigan species have flexible-shelled eggs, but softshells and musk turtles lay hard-shelled eggs; snapping turtle eggs are hard-shelled when first laid but become flexible as incubation progresses.

All turtles and tortoises lay eggs on land. Basic nest construction techniques are remarkably similar for nearly all of them, indicating that this nesting behavior probably dates back to the beginnings of turtles, and perhaps to the beginnings of reptiles. The female turtle uses her hind feet to construct a cavity in sand or soil. The eggs are laid, arranged with the hind feet, and then covered and abandoned to their fate, with the mother turtle never seeing her eggs and probably never seeing her young.

Most Michigan turtles nest in June (the range is from late May through early July). Some species

This turtle nest was destroyed by a raccoon, which left behind only empty eggshells.

(e.g., painted, map, and softshell turtles) may lay two or more clutches per year, while others normally produce a single clutch (e.g., wood turtles). Small turtles generally lay fewer eggs than larger species. Our smallest species (musk, spotted, and box turtles) average fewer than six eggs per year, while a large snapping turtle can lay 60 or more eggs in each nest.

Many turtle eggs (probably a majority) never hatch. Raccoons and skunks are the primary turtle nest raiders in Michigan, but foxes, coyotes, otters, mink, bears, crows, and ravens also take a share. Most egg predators seem to use scent clues to find the nests. The longer a nest escapes detection, the greater are its chances of producing hatchlings. Rain showers may save some nests by washing away the odors left on the surface by the female turtle.

The time it takes a turtle egg to hatch varies with the temperatures and humidity within the nest, but it usually ranges from 60 to 90 days in Michigan. Thus, an egg laid in early June will probably hatch in late August or early September.

The hatchlings break through the eggshell by scratching with their claws and by using a tooth-like projection on their noses called a caruncle. The caruncle is shed soon after hatching. They must then dig to the surface to face a world of turtle-eating predators. Most hatchlings emerge with a lingering supply of yolk in the digestive tract to sustain them in their first days or weeks out of the nest.

In painted turtles, and some other species as well, the baby turtles may remain in the nest throughout the fall and winter and emerge in spring. Temperatures in the nest often fall below freezing, but a natural body "antifreeze" helps keep the young turtles alive. Extremely low temperatures are fatal, however, and survival is best in years with heavy, insulating snow cover.

■ One of the more interesting discoveries about turtles in recent years is that, in some species, the sex of a baby turtle is determined by the nest temperature during an early stage of incubation. Generally, warmer nests produce more females, while cooler nests produce more males. For example, map and painted turtle eggs incubated at 77° F (25°C) hatch into males, while eggs incubated at 87° F (30.5°C) produce females. Eggs kept near a pivotal temperature of about 84° F (29°C) result in both males and females. Snapping turtles have a similar pattern, except that very cool eggs at about 70° F (21°C) as well as warm eggs produce females, while temperatures in-between produce males. While the sex of most Michigan turtles is determined by incubation temperature, the sex of spiny softshells is genetically determined, as in birds and mammals. A study on wood turtles shows that their sex is also independent of egg temperatures.

■ Young turtles grow relatively rapidly for the first few years and then more slowly once they reach maturity. Old turtles may barely grow at all. The length of time needed to reach breeding size varies between species and is also influenced by the turtle's environment. Painted turtles may mature in about five years, snappers in seven or eight years, while wood turtles need about 14 years.

Males and females may differ considerably in maturation times. Male common musk turtles require three to four years to reach breeding size, while females may need eight years or more. The peak breeding years for a turtle may come many years after reaching sexual maturity. For example, a box turtle can mature in about six years, but it might take another 14 years to reach full adult size. Within species, larger females generally lay larger clutches of eggs than do smaller females.

Considering the number of predators that feed on turtle eggs and hatchlings and the very low probability that any turtle egg will eventually produce an adult turtle, it may seem like a miracle that turtles have survived for so many millions of years. But turtles do have one thing going for them — their potentially long lives once they become adults. If a female turtle can produce eggs each spring for a number of years, or even decades, the chances become good that some eggs will hatch and a few offspring will survive. Thus, the key to turtle success has much to do with longevity, and the key to conserving our native turtles is to assure them the chance for long lives.

Notes on Lizard Biology

*L*izards, like turtles, are an ancient group of reptiles. The first primitive lizards appeared in the late Permian period, about 235 million years ago, predating the first dinosaurs. By the late Jurassic period (the middle of the age of dinosaurs), about 140 milion years ago, most of the lizard groups alive today had already appeared, including relatives of Michigan's two species. From their beginnings to the present, most lizards have been rather small animals, usually less than 8 inches (20 cm) long, excluding the tail. During the Cretaceous period (the last part of the age of dinosaurs) one group of lizards, the mosasaurs, evolved a serpent-like shape and paddle-shaped limbs for swimming in the sea and grew to great size, up to 33 feet (10 m) long. Mosasaurs were relatives of the living monitor lizards, one of which, the Asian Komodo dragon, is the largest lizard today, reaching a length of about 10 feet (3 m).

■ Lizards are only distantly related to turtles, but they are more closely related to the extinct dinosaurs and the living crocodiles and alligators. Lizards and snakes are very closely related, and fossil evidence shows that snakes evolved from lizards over 70 million years ago. Some lizard types in Africa and Australia are still in the process of becoming legless, and species of legless lizards live in the eastern United States today. Two features that separate legless lizards from snakes are the presence of eyelids (snakes have window-like scales over the eyes and cannot blink) and external ear openings (nearly all lizards have them, but snakes do not).

There are more than 3700 species of lizards, compared with only about 250 species of turtles. Lizards occur in most of the temperate, subtropical, and tropical parts of the world. In some dry tropical areas they may be the most abundant type of backboned animal. They become less numerous in colder climates. Michigan has only two species, one of which (the five-lined skink) is fairly common while the other (the six-lined racerunner) is extremely rare.

Adaptations and Senses

■ A lizard's body is entirely covered by dry scales, which may be tiny and granular or large and plate-like. The scales may either lie in contact or overlap, and they can be smooth or have ridges called keels. Some lizards have little bony plates under their scales called osteoderms, as in Michigan's five-lined skink.

Unlike the solid skull of a turtle, the lizard skull is not roofed over with bone and is very light and flexible, allowing some movement of the bones when swallowing large objects. Because their lower jaw bones are fused, lizards cannot swallow objects larger than their heads, as snakes do. Lizards usually have lots of small teeth along the jaws and sometimes on the roof of the mouth. The teeth are used to seize and, in some species, to crush their food.

Like snakes, lizards can use their tongues to pick up chemical clues about food sources, potential enemies, or mates. Most species do not flick their tongues out as often as snakes, and it is possible that this chemical sensing is not as important in lizards as it is in snakes. The six-lined racerunner, however, is one species that does make frequent tongue flicks as it walks over the ground. Most lizards have good eyesight.

■ The lizard tail is a very specialized part of its body. Many species shed their tails when seized by a predator, and some shed the tail voluntarily as a predator is approaching. The separated tail wriggles violently, thus attracting the predator's attention while the lizard runs away. This is possible due to special weak points in the tail bones combined with small muscles that pull them apart. After tail separation, the blood vessels contract to limit blood loss, and in a few weeks a new tail grows. The replacement tail is often shorter and less colorful than the original. Some lizards use their tails for fat storage, and the loss of the tail may reduce the energy reserves available for reproduction or winter survivial.

Most lizards bite if grabbed, but the only poisonous species are the beaded lizard and the Gila monster of the southwestern United States and Mexico. Michigan's lizards do little more than offer a mild pinch if handled and prefer to escape enemies by hiding or running.

Like turtles and other reptiles, lizards obtain the warmth they need for normal activity from their environment, especially by basking in the sun. Lizards can "fine-tune" their body temperature by changing their position in relation to the sun or moving in or out of the shade. During winter they use burrows or other shelters to escape freezing temperatures and become dormant until spring.

Finding Food

■ Most lizards are predators, with the great majority feeding on small invertebrates such as insects and spiders. The prey is usually seized with the jaws and crushed with the teeth before it is swallowed. There are some herbivorous (plant-eating) lizards, such as the green iguana of Mexico, and Central and South America, and the chuckawalla of the western United States. Michigan's two species generally eat insects, though five-lined skinks reportedly eat berries on occasion.

Reproductive Behavior

■ Lizards have complex social behaviors that are mostly related to reproduction. The males of many species will use visual displays to intimidate rivals or attract females. The common green anole of the southern United States extends its bright red throat fan, called a dewlap, and performs a head-bobbing push-up display for these purposes. Male five-lined skinks develop reddish heads during the breeding season and chase other red-headed males from their territories while allowing the blue-tailed females and juveniles to stay.

Courting males often use behaviors similar to territorial displays as part of the courtship ritual. For mating to occur, a female must identify herself as the proper species and perform ritual behaviors of her own to convey a willingness to mate. Fertilization is internal. A male lizard has a double penis, the hemipenes, and only one of the hemipenes is used for each mating.

Most female lizards produce eggs, which are usually oval with a leathery, flexible shell. In egg-laying species, eggs are usually deposited in a cavity underneath a rock or log or in a burrow dug by the female. In a few species, including the five-lined skink, the female will stay with the eggs during incubation, keeping them moist and providing protection from small predators. Often some embryonic development occurs before the eggs are laid, and females of some species retain the embryos throughout their development and the young are born alive.

In any case there is little or no care of the young, which usually disperse rapidly after hatching. Baby lizards are basically miniatures of the adults. They hatch out as tiny, active creatures ready to feed and care for themselves.

■ A few kinds of lizards occur in all-female populations. They are able to lay eggs which, though unfertilized by males, develop successfully into new female lizards. Some of these single-sex lizard species are closely related to the six-lined racerunner that breeds in Michigan. The all-female lizards may be able to successfully invade new habitats better than most species, since it takes only one lizard to start a new colony, and they can reproduce rapidly. Because all of the lizards in the colony would be genetically alike, however, they may be less able to adapt to environmental changes than normal lizard species with males and females.

Compared with turtles, most lizards grow and mature more rapidly, and individuals of many species can reproduce at an age of one year or less. Their lives are typically much shorter than turtles', and few lizards survive more than a decade. A four-year-old skink is an old lizard, but a four-year-old wood turtle is a youngster, perhaps 10 years from maturity!

Studying Turtles and Lizards Outdoors and Indoors

The best way to study turtles and lizards is to watch them in the wild. Many species can be easily observed under natural conditions, if the observer is patient and remains still. Basking or foraging turtles or lizards normally flee if they detect a potentially threatening movement. But a person who finds a partly concealed spot and sits quietly, perhaps with binoculars or camera at the ready, can be rewarded with views of the many fascinating behaviors displayed by these animals.

When turtles or lizards are captured and put in confined spaces, their behavior changes. At first, most specimens try to escape. They may eventually settle down and adapt to captive conditions, but one can never be certain that their actions are truly normal. Scientists who study wild animals in the laboratory know that the behavior of captive specimens may not necessarily reflect what happens in the wild. Situations do exist in which keeping a turtle or lizard in captivity may provide educational benefits. School science classrooms, nature centers, and summer camps are places where displays of common species may be useful.

■ **Before keeping any turtle or lizard, ask these questions:**

☐ Is there a good reason to remove the animal from the wild and keep it captive?

☐ Is it legal? *In Michigan, eastern box, spotted, and wood turtles are protected by law, and other species have* *possession limits, size limits, and closed seasons. (Check with the DNR for current regulations.) Remember that a fishing license is needed to take unprotected turtles for personal use. Never capture or purchase a specimen if there is any doubt about its legality.* Even if a species is not protected, don't collect them if they seem uncommon in the local area.*

☐ Does the species or specimen present special care problems? *(Recommended species are noted on page 87.)*

☐ Can you provide a suitable, healthy environment for the animal? *(See needs on page 87.)*

☐ When the time comes to release the specimen, can it be returned to its original habitat? *(Specimens released in strange territory, even if the habitat seems suitable, may have a poor chance to survive.)*

*NOTE: The authors discourage purchasing wild-caught reptiles from pet dealers or biological supply firms. Collecting reptiles, particularly in commercial quantities, can damage wild populations.

Guidelines for Care of Captive Turtles

Species easiest to keep include painted turtles, red-eared sliders, musk turtles, and small snapping turtles. Softshells and map turtles have special housing and dietary needs that make them difficult captives. These two, and Blanding's turtles, are also very active and require more room than many people can provide. Large snapping turtles are potentially dangerous in confined situations.

The following information applies to the captive care of the hardy species previously noted. Your turtle needs: water (for swimming, feeding), warmth (a range of 75° to 85°F is good), a place to dry off (a basking spot), and a nutritious diet.

Housing: Standard glass aquaria and plastic storage boxes work well. Containers must be watertight and escape-proof. A loose-fitting cover is recommended to hold in warmth and humidity.

Water: Most tap water is suitable for turtles. Depth depends on specimen size. They should be able to swim freely but not need to struggle to reach the surface. Keep it clean! Pet shops sell power filters for larger tanks. Small tanks can be cleaned by dumping and filling, as often as necessary. Avoid sudden temperature changes.

Dry spot: Provide a dry, warm spot that turtles can climb easily. A smooth rock is fine. For larger tanks,

sloping ramps can be made of plastic or untreated wood. Position a 40 to 60 watt incandescent light over the basking area to provide a hot spot of about 80° F (27°C). Make sure turtles cannot touch the bulb or fixture.
Note: *Direct sun is beneficial, but provide shade and guard against overheating.*

Temperature: Water can be cooler than the basking spot. Turtles should be able to choose temperatures within a range of about 75° to 85°F (24° to 30°C). Temperatures over 90° F (32° C) or under 70° F (21° C) for extended periods can harm turtles. We recommend releasing captives in early autumn, while they can still find a suitable place to hibernate. If kept over winter, turtles must have summer temperatures. Normal room temperatures of 65° to 70° F are not suitable. Hibernating captive turtles is possible but involves some risks and is not advised except for research purposes.

Feeding: Most turtles, including all of the noted hardy species, must swallow food with their heads underwater. Suitable foods for captives include small whole or chopped fish, earthworms, soft-bodied insects (do not feed flies or ants), and lean bits of beef heart or liver (but not hamburger or raw poultry). Some species also eat dark green leafy vegetables (Romaine, elodea, etc., but not head lettuce). Certain commercial food pellets, such as Reptomin® and Purina Trout Chow® are acceptable, but do not purchase so-called turtle food containing dried flies or ant pupae, as they are not nutritious. Turtles have a special need for such nutrients as calcium and vitamins A and D_3.

When keeping specimens for long periods, it is a good idea to add a powdered or liquid vitamin and mineral supplement (available at pet and feed stores) to the food once or twice per week.

Feeding hints: Feed turtles in a separate container to cut down on cleaning and the chance of contamination. This also makes it easier to keep track of how much they eat. Keep food pieces small. Small turtles can be fed daily; larger turtles three to four times per week.

Growth and health: A healthy young turtle is alert, feeds readily and grows rapidly (an inch or more per year). Older juveniles and adults grow more slowly. Most illness in captive turtles is the result of poor diet or low temperatures. If a turtle refuses to eat, is lethargic, does not grow properly, or shows any other signs of not adapting to captive conditions, release it where you found it before it develops serious health problems!

Turtles and the Salmonella problem: The U.S. Food and Drug Administration has banned the sale of baby turtles (under 4 inches in shell length) because it was found that, under certain circumstances, turtles carry *Salmonella* bacteria, which can cause food poisoning symptoms in humans. The problem largely occurred when children received baby turtles bought from pet shops but did not know how to properly care for them. These turtles (usually red-eared sliders) were often kept under unsanitary conditions before the sale and then poorly treated after being brought into the home. This resulted in sickly turtles living in dirty water and being handled by children who often placed fingers (and sometimes turtles!) in their mouths. Unfortunately, some people reading media accounts mistakenly assumed that all turtles were diseased and dangerous. There is little chance of catching any disease from a healthy, well-kept, wild-caught turtle. Most *Salmonella* poisoning probably results from poorly stored food and raw eggs or poultry.

It is always advisable to wash your hands after handling any pet. Turtle tanks should not be cleaned in kitchen sinks or near food preparation areas.

Please note: turtles are **not** suitable pets for small children. Turtles are not toys and do not have any need for play. Do not handle captive turtles except when necessary for maintaining their health and environment.

Guidelines for Care of Captive Lizards

The only native Michigan lizard suitable for an educational exhibit is the five-lined skink. The six-lined racerunner is extremely rare in Michigan, and any seen in the wild should not be disturbed.

Lizards are more fragile animals than most turtles and should be collected with great care, and then only for scientific or educational purposes.

Most lizards require live insects as food—a factor to be considered before obtaining a specimen.

Housing: A terrarium for a skink could be an empty aquarium tank with a tight-fitting screened top. An easily cleaned or replaced bottom surface such as artificial grass or smooth gravel can be used, with irregular pieces of bark placed on it to provide hiding places and basking perches. A shallow water dish should always be available. Some lizards, such as the green anole (American chameleon) of the southern states, prefer to drink from small droplets rather than a dish.

Heat: The temperature ranges previously described for turtles are probably suitable for skinks, though these lizards may prefer slightly higher basking temperatures — perhaps 85° F (29°C). An incandescent light focused on one end of the terrarium can provide a necessary hot spot for basking, while the cooler end allows the captives a choice of temperatures. Nighttime temperatures can be lower.

Feeding: Skinks feed largely on live insects, which can be obtained in the summer months by sweeping grassy areas with an insect collecting net. Avoid houseflies and ants. Flies carry disease bacteria and ants are not eaten by most lizards. Some skinks will reportedly feed on bits of dog food and boiled egg yolk offered in a dish, but most lizards refuse food that isn't moving.

It is recommended that lizard specimens be released into their habitat well before the onset of cold weather in fall. Feeding these animals in winter requires raising or buying insect food, such as crickets or mealworms. Store-bought insects may not be as nutritious as those caught in the wild, and dusting these insects with a powdered vitamin and mineral supplement before feeding them to the lizard may be necessary.

FOR MORE INFORMATION

The following publications *are recommended to readers seeking additional information on turtles and lizards of the Great Lakes area and reptiles in general.*

Behler, J.L., and F.W. King. 1979. *The Audubon Society Field Guide to North American Reptiles and Amphibians.* New York: Alfred A. Knopf, Inc. 719 pp.

Conant, R. 1975. *A Field Guide to Reptiles and Amphibians of Eastern and Central North America.* Boston: Houghton Mifflin Co. 429 pp.

Ernst, C.H., and R.W. Barbour. 1972. *Turtles of the United States.* Lexington: Univ. Press of Kentucky. i-x+ 347 pp.

Halliday, T.R., and K. Adler (Eds.). 1986. *The Encyclopedia of Reptiles and Amphibians.* New York: Facts On File, Inc. 152 pp.

Holman, J.A., J.H. Harding, M.M. Hensley, and G.R. Dudderar. 1989. *Michigan Snakes.* East Lansing: Cooperative Extension Serv., Michigan State Univ. Bull. E-2000. 72 pp.

Minton, S.A. 1972. *Amphibians and Reptiles of Indiana.* Indianapolis: Indiana Acad. of Science. Monograph No. 3. 346 pp.

Ruthven, A.G., C. Thompson, and H.T. Gaige. 1928. *The Herpetology of Michigan.* Ann Arbor: University Museums, The Univ. of Michigan. Handbook Ser. No. 3.

Smith, P.W. 1961. *The Amphibians and Reptiles of Illinois.* Bull. Illinois Nat. Hist. Survey. Vol. 28. 298 pp.

Vogt, R.C. 1981. *Natural History of Amphibians and Reptiles of Wisconsin.* Milwaukee: Milwaukee Public Museum. 205 pp.